THE

UNDERWATER

WORLD

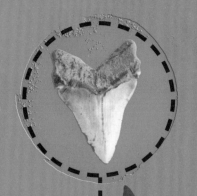

OF

SHARKS

This edition published by Parragon Books Ltd in 2016 and distributed by

Parragon Inc.
440 Park Avenue South, 13th Floor
New York, NY 10016
www.parragon.com

Edited by Grace Harvey
Cover design by Elizabeth Doyle
Production by Charlene Vaughan
Designed and produced by Tall Tree Ltd

ISBN 978-1-4748-2988-5

Printed in China

THE
UNDERWATER
WORLD
OF
SHARKS

PaRragon

Bath · New York · Cologne · Melbourne · Delhi
Hong Kong · Shenzhen · Singapore

INTRODUCTION

Sharks are found in all the oceans of the world.
Some are fierce meat-eaters that rip their prey
to shreds, others feed on tiny plants and animals,
called plankton, that drift along in the ocean currents.

Our planet was formed around 4.5 billion years
ago. The first living creatures appeared roughly
1.2 billion years later. Life in the oceans evolved
slowly, until sharks appeared around 400 million
years ago. Since then, sharks have evolved into
over 470 different species.

The longest existing modern sharks are the
cow sharks (sixgill and sevengill), which date
back 190 million years. These primitive species
can be found in the deep sea. The newest
modern sharks are the hammerheads, which
are thought to date back 50 million years.
Sharks are among the oldest creatures that have
been living continuously on Earth.

The term *shark* was first used in 1569 to
advertise a specimen that was brought back
to London, England, and exhibited there.
Sailors had caught it during an expedition to
South America commanded by the famous
Elizabethan seaman Captain John Hawkins.
Why the sailors called this fish a "shark" remains
a mystery.

Sharks live in various marine habitats around
the world. Most prefer temperate and tropical
waters, but some are found in colder seas near
the North and South Poles. They range from
the shallow waters near the coastline right out
to the open ocean, and some even live in deep
waters where light does not reach.

WHAT IS A SHARK?

Sharks are fish that live in the seas and oceans all over the world. There are over 470 different species of shark. They have been living on Earth for 400 million years. The shape of a shark is so perfectly adapted to living in the water that it hasn't changed much in all that time.

DIFFERENT TYPES OF SHARK

Some sharks are tiny, others are giants. Some are gentle, and some are fierce. Some swim very fast to catch their prey in the open sea. Others move slowly and feed on animals that live on the ocean floor.

Fin
Stiff fins are supported by rods of cartilage.

Gills
Gills are used to breathe.

Snout
The snout is often sharply pointed. The mouth is shaped like a crescent.

DISCOVERY FACT™

Inside most fish is an air-filled swim bladder, which keeps the fish afloat. Sharks don't have swim bladders. Instead, they have oil-filled livers that help them float. Most, however, have to keep swimming or they sink.

Dogfish have long, slim bodies to slip through the water.

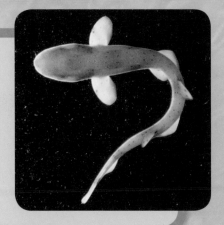

Wobbegongs hide on the seabed. They are well camouflaged.

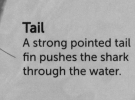

Tail
A strong pointed tail fin pushes the shark through the water.

Angel sharks have flat bodies. They also hide on the seabed.

Basking sharks live in open water. They are often seen swimming very close to the coastline.

AMAZING SHARKS

Can you imagine a fish that has a head shaped like a hammer? Or one that can gobble up a sea lion whole? Sharks are some of the world's most amazing creatures.

Great white shark

The great white shark eats other sharks for dinner—along with whole penguins, seals, and sea lions.

Whale shark

The gentle whale shark is the world's biggest fish. It weighs as much as two elephants and can grow longer than a bus.

Mako shark

The bullet-shaped mako shark can swim at over 43 miles per hour. It is one of the fastest fish in the ocean.

Hammerhead shark

The hammerhead shark has eyes on each side of its head. It swings its head from side to side to get an all-around view.

Hammerhead sharks have smaller pectoral fins than other species of shark.

DISCOVERY FACT™

Sharks don't have bones. Their skeletons are made from light, stretchy cartilage. This is the same kind of material that humans have in their ears and noses.

TEETH

Teeth are a shark's most important weapon. They are designed to help it catch and eat prey.

Sharks have multiple rows of teeth. Every time a shark loses a tooth, the tooth in the row behind it moves forward to take the lost tooth's place.

The shape of a shark's tooth depends on its diet. Sharks that eat fish have long, narrow teeth for gripping slippery fish. Sharks that eat mammals such as seal, have sharp, jagged teeth for ripping flesh. Sharks that eat shellfish have thick, platelike teeth to crush the shells of their prey.

Sharks' teeth are not rooted in the jaw like ours, but are attached to the skin covering the jaw.

Unlike most animals' jaws, both the shark's upper and lower jaws move. It bites with its lower jaw first and then its upper.

The great white shark has sharp, pointy teeth, perfect for ripping flesh.

The prehistoric shark Megalodon may have been up to 65 feet long. Here is one of its huge teeth next to the tooth of a modern shark.

The powerful tail of a great white shark helps propel it through the water, to attack prey.

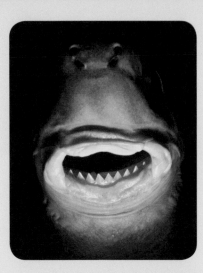

The small cookiecutter shark swims up to a larger fish, takes a bite out of its side (the shape of a cookie), and swims away again very quickly!

HOW SHARKS SWIM

Dorsal fin
The stiff fin on a shark's back helps with balance.

Most sharks are graceful and powerful swimmers. Their smooth bodies are perfect for moving underwater. Sharks swim in S-shaped movements, powered by their tails.

Tail
The shark's tail is a little bit like its motor. It sweeps it from side to side in long strokes, powering its body forward. The streamlined shape of the shark's body helps it glide through the water. Sharks with large tails can accelerate very quickly.

Pectoral fins
Fins on each side of a shark's body help it steer.

Fins
The dorsal fin on the shark's back acts like the keel of a boat. It stops the shark from rolling over in the water. The pectoral fins on the sides help to move the shark up and down in the water, like the wings of an aircraft.

DISCOVERY FACT™

Sharks cannot swim backward. This is because a shark's stiff pectoral fins cannot bend upward (unlike those of most other fish), so they are unable to back up.

Tail

A shark's long tail beats from side to side, pushing the shark forward through the water.

Types of tail

The caudal, or tail, fins of sharks vary a lot in shape and size. The top half of the fin is usually larger than the bottom half because the shark's backbone extends into the upper half of the fin.

Tiger shark

Nurse shark

Porbeagle

Thresher shark

Great white shark

Cookiecutter shark

Slow motion

Whale sharks are slow swimmers, cruising along at about 3 miles per hour. They swim by moving their entire bodies from side to side, not just their tails.

Thresher shark

The thresher shark has the longest tail of any shark—its upper part is almost as long as the rest of the shark's body. When hunting fish, thresher sharks are known to "slap" the water with their tail to stun their prey before eating it.

SENSES AND HUNTING

Sharks are always seeking out their next meal. They can see, hear, touch, and smell, just like people. But their senses are much more powerful than ours and are perfectly adapted to working in water.

Touch

Finding food

A shark uses all its senses to find prey, but smell gives it some of the most important clues. A shark can smell a tiny amount of blood in the water from hundreds of feet away.

Touch

A lateral line along their sides helps sharks pick up movements in the water around them.

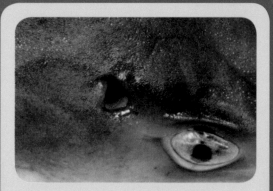

Hearing

A shark's ears can hear sounds traveling through the water. The ears lie beneath small holes in the shark's head.

Extra sense

Sharks have special jelly-filled receptors in their heads. These extra sense organs let sharks pick up the faint electric signals given off by fish. This sense is particularly powerful in hammerhead sharks.

Sight

Smell

Hearing

Sight

A shark's eyes can see well in dim underwater light.

Smell

A shark does not breathe through its nose. It is just used for detecting smell.

MOTHERS AND PUPS

All baby sharks are born from eggs and are known as pups. The eggs of most sharks grow inside their mother. A few kinds of shark lay their eggs on the seabed, safe inside tough egg cases.

All sharks are born from eggs that are fertilized by sperm from the male shark. But the eggs can grow in different ways. In some sharks, they remain inside the mother's body and hatch inside her. The young shark pups are then born as live fish, ready to swim away.

Other sharks lay their eggs inside tough, leathery egg cases in the water. The pup grows inside the egg case feeding on the yolk inside it. When it is ready to be born, the young shark wriggles its way out of the case, which splits open.

Little hammerheads
Baby hammerhead sharks are born with their heads bent backward, so they don't get stuck inside their mother.

Egg cases
Dogfish eggs are protected by an egg case called a mermaid's purse. The babies grow inside, feeding on the egg yolk.

DISCOVERY FACT™

A blue shark mother can give birth to 50 or more babies at a time. The record for this shark is 135 pups. They take 9 to 12 months to grow big enough to be born.

Groups of sharks

Sharks do not remain in a family group. When sharks are seen together in a large group, it is usually because a lot of food is available to be eaten.

Lemon sharks

Lemon shark eggs grow inside their mother. She gives birth to tiny pups, which soon swim off to find food. They remain in fairly shallow water while they grow to their adult size of almost 7 feet long. This can take between 12 and 15 years.

THE SHARK'S WORLD

Our Earth is often called the blue planet because more than two-thirds of its surface is covered by water. Most of this water is found in the oceans. This is where the sharks have their home. They live in shallow waters around the world's coasts and in deeper water all the way down to the ocean floor.

THE OCEANS

There are five oceans. The largest is the Pacific Ocean, which stretches between North and South America, Australia, and the eastern coast of Asia. The smallest is the Arctic Ocean, which surrounds the North Pole. All five of the world's oceans are connected. Smaller areas of water, called seas, are joined to some of the oceans. These include the Caribbean, Mediterranean, and North Seas.

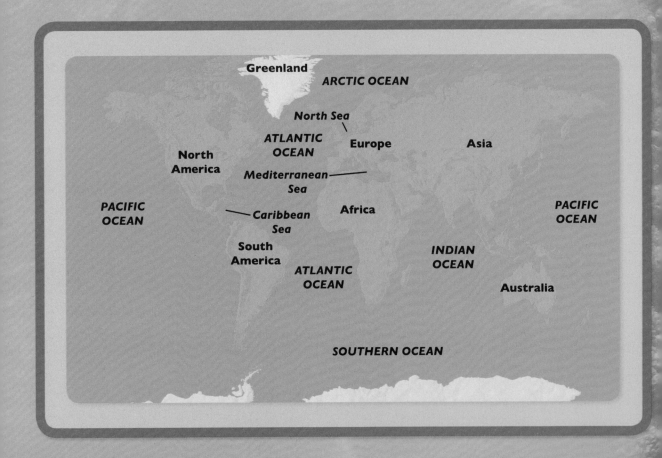

Greenland

ARCTIC OCEAN

North Sea

ATLANTIC OCEAN

Europe

Asia

North America

Mediterranean Sea

PACIFIC OCEAN

Caribbean Sea

Africa

PACIFIC OCEAN

South America

INDIAN OCEAN

ATLANTIC OCEAN

Australia

SOUTHERN OCEAN

Ocean islands

Oceans are mostly wide, open areas of water. Islands are scattered across the oceans. These pieces of land rise up from under the water. Islands may cover large areas of land or just a few square miles.

A small island in the Indian Ocean.

Coral reefs

Coral reefs are found off coasts and around islands in tropical parts of the world. Reefs are home to many kinds of fish, including reef sharks, and other colorful marine animals.

Coral reefs are built from the skeletons of tiny sea animals.

DISCOVERY FACT™

Sharks play an important role in keeping our oceans healthy. Most sharks are at the top of the food chain, and they eat old or sick marine animals. The animals that survive are the fittest ones.

SHARKS IN ANCIENT TIMES

Humans have been exploring the world by sea for thousands of years. Sharks have always been a danger to people whose work takes them out onto or into the ocean. Nearly 2000 years ago, the ancient Roman author Pliny wrote about sharks attacking men who were diving for sponges.

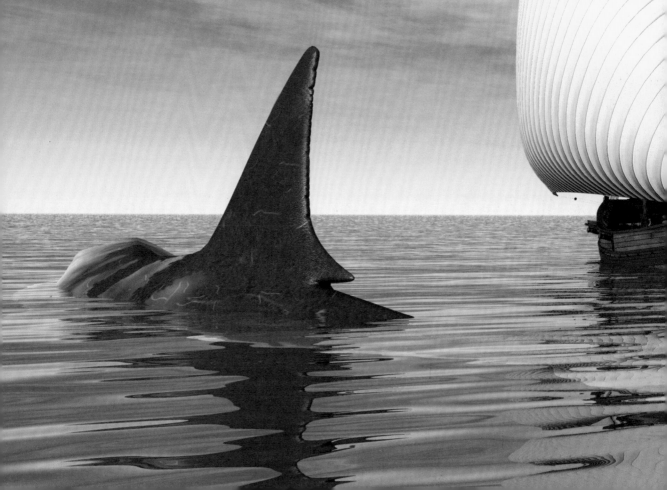

Hawaiian myth

Sharks have been both feared and worshiped by human beings since ancient times. In Hawaiian myth, a shark god created the universe and everything in it.

Ancient bond

Humans have collected sharks' teeth for thousands of years. People used to believe they would give some of the unique predatory abilities of sharks.

DISCOVERY FACT.™

When the dinosaurs' cousins, the plesiosaurs, went extinct, prehistoric sharks became the main predators in the oceans. They have evolved into the sharks we know today.

BULL SHARK

The bull shark is a fierce predator that will eat almost anything that it comes across. It is solitary, usually choosing to hunt by itself.

The bull shark is large and has a wide body in relation to its length. It is colored gray on top and off-white below.

It is one of the few sharks that can live in freshwater. Bull sharks are often seen in rivers and lakes. One was even spotted 2,480 miles upstream in the Amazon River in Iquitos, Peru.

Bull sharks eat all kinds of animals in the water, and this includes other sharks, especially the sandbar shark. They sometimes use a "bump and bite" technique, headbutting their victim first before biting it.

Bull sharks are one of the most dangerous sharks to humans because they are aggressive and often come into shallow coastal waters where people swim and surf. Many of the recorded attacks on people have been made by bull sharks.

Snout
This is wider than it is long, which is unusual for a shark.

Body
The bull shark has a much wider body in relation to its length than most other sharks.

Profile

Length:	Average 7 ft (males), 11.5 ft (females)
Weight:	Average 200 lb (males), 287 lb (females)
Order:	Ground sharks
Family:	Requiem sharks
Diet:	Fish (including other sharks), dolphins, turtles, birds, invertebrates

Location

Bull sharks are found worldwide in the coastal waters of tropical and subtropical (more than 64 °F) seas and sometimes in rivers. They swim from the surface to about 100 feet deep.

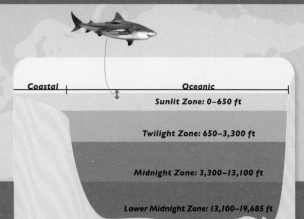

Coastal | Oceanic

Sunlit Zone: 0–650 ft

Twilight Zone: 650–3,300 ft

Midnight Zone: 3,300–13,100 ft

Lower Midnight Zone: 13,100–19,685 ft

SALT WATER

Seawater tastes very salty. This is because the water contains a lot of dissolved salt. Humans cannot drink seawater because it makes them sick. But animals that live in the sea have ways of coping with the high levels of salt.

Coping with salty water

Sharks can get rid of any excess salt that they ingest. A gland at the end of the intestine absorbs salt from the blood, and it is then excreted.

Adding more salt

Some of the salt in seawater is made when rocks break down, and from hot-water vents on the ocean floor. Volcanic eruptions underwater also add salt to the oceans.

Clouds of steam pour from an undersea volcanic eruption.

Sharks have evolved to live in seawater.

Turtle tears

Turtles have a salt gland behind their eyes. By getting rid of salt through their eyes, nostrils, or tongue, turtles can live in salt water without becoming ill.

Salt pans

When salt water gathers in shallow ponds, the water dries up, leaving behind large areas of salt called salt pans. The salt can be collected and used for cooking.

DISCOVERY FACT™

The water in the Dead Sea in the Middle East is ten times saltier than in the oceans. This is because the sea has no outlets (such as rivers or streams). This means the salt cannot be carried away.

Dry salt is left when the water evaporates.

LIVING IN WATER

Animals that live in water are called aquatic animals. Their bodies are adapted to life in water. Fish have gills to breathe underwater, while seals have flippers to help them swim.

Gills are used to breathe.

Sharks

Sharks are fish, and they breathe using gills. Water enters through their mouths and passes through the gills, where the oxygen is removed. The oxygen goes into the shark's bloodstream and is pumped around the body by the heart. The water is pumped out of the shark's body through the gill slits back into the sea.

DISCOVERY FACT™

Some sharks are not able to pass water through their gills unless they keep swimming forward. This means they cannot rest, but must spend their whole lives swimming in order to breathe.

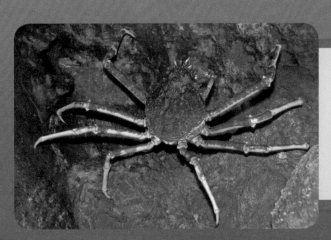

Crabs

A crab has a heavy outer skeleton covering its body. The crab's body is flat so that it can easily squeeze under and between rocks. Crabs have gills inside their shells and can breathe underwater like fish.

Jellyfish

Jellyfish have a soft body made mostly of water. They must stay in water to keep their shape. If you take a jellyfish out of the water, it will collapse into a blob of jelly (like a gelatin dessert).

Seals

Seals are marine mammals with flippers instead of arms and legs. Although seals live in water, they breathe air and have to return to land to give birth.

Seals have to come up to the surface to breathe air.

FOOD CHAINS

A food chain shows how nutrients pass from plants to animals as one eats the other. In the ocean, plant plankton is eaten by animal plankton, or zooplankton. The zooplankton is eaten by larger animals. These animals are then eaten by even bigger animals. Many sharks have a diet of seals, turtles, fish, and even large seabirds. Some sharks, however, such as the whale shark and basking shark, eat plankton and small fish.

Plant plankton

Plant plankton are at the bottom of the ocean food chains. They are called producers because they make their own food using sunlight.

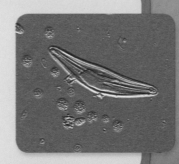

Top meat-eaters

Top carnivores, or meat-eaters, such as pelicans, sharks, and dolphins, eat fish. A top carnivore is an animal that no other animal eats—they are at the top of the ocean food chain.

Plant-eaters

Zooplankton, or plant-eaters, such as this crab larva, eat the producers, or plant plankton. The plant-eaters are known as primary consumers.

Meat-eaters

Larger animals called the secondary consumers eat the primary consumers. Secondary consumers are hunters. There are many different hunters in the ocean, including fish and squid.

This great white shark has leaped out of the water to catch a seal.

The darker shade of this shark's back blends with the sea, so that it can attack prey from below.

DISCOVERY FACT™

The great white shark attacks its prey from below. It swims until it is only a few yards away, then attacks by turning its head upward and surging up through the water.

BENEATH THE SURFACE

Imagine if you could walk into the sea from a beach. First, you would walk through the shallow water of the continental shelf that extends out from the coast. Then, the seabed slopes down for thousands of feet to the deep ocean floor.

Ocean levels

In some places the continental shelf is narrow, but in others it stretches for hundreds of miles. The continental slope links the continental shelf with the ocean floor, which may be thousands of feet down.

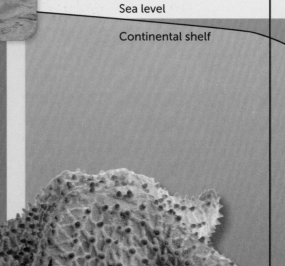

Sea level

Continental shelf

Sea lions

Sea lions swim in the shallow water close to the shore above the continental shelf. They like to pull themselves out of the water and lie on sandy beaches.

Starfish

Starfish are found on the continental shelf. They crawl over the sand hunting for mussels and other shellfish to eat.

The deepest-known part of the ocean is the Mariana Trench in the Pacific Ocean. It lies 6.8 miles below sea level.

Wide-set eyes help the hammerhead shark see above and below at all times.

Hammerhead shark

Sharks, such as this hammerhead shark, are found in both shallow and deep water. Some sharks can dive down several thousand feet to the bottom of the oceans.

Different creatures are found at each depth of the ocean.

Spider crab

Spider crabs are creatures of the seabed. They have been found on the ocean floor more than 10,000 feet below the water's surface.

Continental slope

Ocean floor

TIGER SHARK

Tiger sharks get their name from the stripes and spots that cover the bodies of their young. It also reflects their reputation as large and powerful hunters of the seas.

Tiger sharks are gray-brown on top with a light yellow to white underside. These sharks are some of the largest predatory fish in the seas—the biggest can grow up to 18 feet long and weigh more than 1,760 pounds.

Tiger sharks have been called "the garbage cans" of the oceans, since they will eat almost anything. Strange items such as tires, bottles, rolls of chicken wire, and even a crocodile's head have been found in the stomachs of dead tiger sharks.

These sharks are solitary hunters, mostly searching for food at night. They generally swim quite slowly when hunting prey, but they can put in a rapid burst of speed for a vital few seconds when they want to launch an attack.

Teeth
Teeth have sharp, jagged edges that can tear and rip virtually anything—even the shells of turtles.

Profile

Length:	Average 10.5 ft (males), 9.5 ft (females)
Weight:	850–1,400 lb (males and females)
Order:	Ground sharks
Family:	Requiem sharks
Diet:	Fish (including other sharks), turtles, crabs, clams, dolphins, seals, seabirds

Tail fin
The upper part of the tail fin is very long—perfect for swimming quickly as the shark moves in for the kill.

Location
The tiger shark is found worldwide in tropical (more than 64 °F) and some temperate (50–64 °F) waters, from the shoreline to the open sea. They swim from the surface to about 1,115 feet deep.

Coastal | Oceanic

Sunlit Zone: 0–650 ft

Twilight Zone: 650–3,300 ft

Midnight Zone: 3,300–13,100 ft

Lower Midnight Zone: 13,100–19,685 ft

DIVING WITH SHARKS

People cannot live in water, but they can dive underwater, using special equipment to help them breathe.

Shark cages allow divers to get very close to large sharks without putting themselves in danger. The sharks are attracted to the cage by the presence of dead fish bait. However, sharks do sometimes show signs of aggression and may attack the cage.

Shark cage

Discovering wrecks
Shipwrecks in shallow water are popular dive sites. By exploring a wreck, divers can learn a lot about the history of the ship.

Exploring reefs

Many divers like to explore coral reefs. These are good places to find brightly colored fish and other marine creatures, such as dolphins and sea turtles.

DISCOVERY FACT™

Sharks are not normally aggressive around divers. If a shark gets too close to a diver, it is sometimes possible to scare it away just by pushing on its nose, which is very sensitive.

Breathing underwater

Scuba divers carry a tank of air to help them breathe underwater. The tank is connected to a regulator, which the diver places in his or her mouth. When the diver breathes in, air flows through the regulator into the mouth.

Regulator

COASTAL SHARKS

The shallow waters around land are full of life. Here, tiny plants called phytoplankton and animals called zooplankton float in the water. Amazingly, the two biggest sharks of all feed on these tiny organisms.

PLANKTON FEEDERS

Animal and plant plankton are the favorite food of many animals, including ocean giants such as the whale shark and basking shark. Most plankton feeders filter, or sieve, tiny organisms from the water.

Basking shark

The basking shark swims along with its mouth wide open. When its mouth is full of water, the fish closes it and squeezes the water out through its gill slits. Any food is trapped inside by rakers (bristle-like filters) in the gills.

Manta ray

Most rays live on the seabed, hunting fish and small animals. The huge manta ray is different. It is an active fish that swims great distances, filtering plankton through its gills.

DISCOVERY FACT™

Scientists believe that some whale sharks may live for up to 180 years. Male whale sharks are not ready to start breeding until they are around 30 years old.

Whale shark

The whale shark is the largest fish in the world. It usually grows up to 40 feet long and can weigh more than 22 tons. It is a filter feeder, and despite its size, it is not a dangerous shark to humans.

Humpback whales have frilly plates in their mouths that sieve the water.

A whale shark's spots are unique and can be used to identify an individual shark, like a human fingerprint.

BASKING SHARK

This incredible-looking shark is the second largest fish (after the whale shark) in the oceans. It may look frightening, but this is a gentle giant. It feeds on tiny plankton as it cruises slowly near the surface.

The body of the basking shark is grayish brown to dark gray, sometimes with lighter patches on the flanks. Its head is quite pointed, but as soon as the shark starts to feed, its appearance changes dramatically. Its huge jaws gape open to allow water to pour over the gill rakers inside its throat. These trap the tiny particles of plankton on which it feeds. This is called filter feeding. More than 343,000 gallons of water—enough to fill two Olympic-sized swimming pools—pass over its bristly gill rakers every hour.

Basking sharks feed near the surface where the tiny plankton organisms are attracted to the sunlight. Fishermen see them fairly often off the coastline. Basking sharks migrate thousands of miles during the winter months, seeking clouds of plankton (called blooms) in warmer waters.

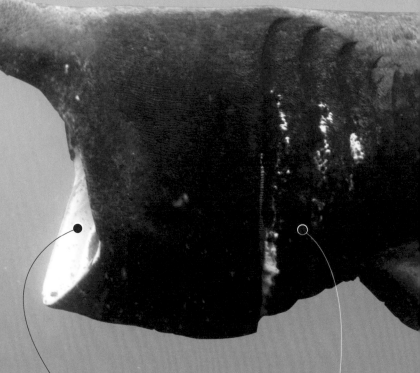

Mouth
A huge mouth like an enormous butterfly net sweeps up tiny food organisms in the water.

Large gill slits
Bristles behind the gill slits, called gill rakers, trap food particles in the water.

Profile

Length:	13–16 ft (males), 24.5–29.5 ft (females)
Weight:	Up to 8,600 lb (males and females)
Order:	Mackerel sharks
Family:	Basking sharks
Diet:	Phytoplankton, zooplankton, tiny fish, fish eggs

Location

The basking shark is found in temperate (50–64 °F) and subpolar (below 50 °F) waters of the North and South Atlantic and Pacific Oceans. They swim from the ocean surface to about 1,870 feet deep.

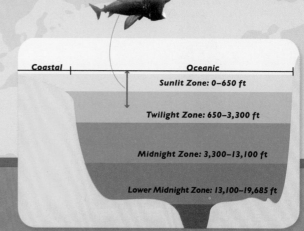

Coastal | Oceanic

Sunlit Zone: 0–650 ft

Twilight Zone: 650–3,300 ft

Midnight Zone: 3,300–13,100 ft

Lower Midnight Zone: 13,100–19,685 ft

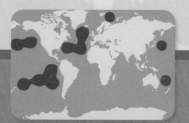

KRILL

Krill are among the most important animals in the ocean. There are billions of these small, shrimplike animals. They are eaten by sharks, whales, seals, penguins, and seabirds.

Krill

Living in numbers
Krill live in large groups, called swarms. Up to 30,000 krill can be found in a cubic yard of water. The wriggling swarm confuses hunters.

Squid
Squid catch krill using their long tentacles. Their sharp beaks rip the krill into small pieces for swallowing.

Penguin predator
Krill are an important food for penguins. Chinstrap penguins feed on larger types of krill, while other species of penguin prefer the smaller ones. Penguins, together with whales, seals, and other seabirds, eat about 165–330 million tons of krill each year.

Whale shark

Whale shark feeding

When they come across swarms of krill, whale sharks hurry to get at the food. They lunge at the krill and churn up the surface of the water as they gulp them into their mouths.

DISCOVERY FACT™

Whale sharks are huge, so they have to eat a lot of food to survive. Scientists measured what one young whale shark was eating. It was more than 46 pounds of food every day.

LEOPARD SHARK

Leopard sharks are one of the most common sharks along the coast of California. They live in shallow waters of the bays and estuaries, and they occasionally patrol the kelp forest, usually staying near the bottom.

This handsomely marked shark has silvery-bronze skin that is covered with darker oval spots. These markings are what give it its name. The older a leopard shark is, the paler the spots will be.

Large schools of leopard sharks are a common sight in bays and estuaries. They swim over sandy or muddy flats or rock-strewn areas near kelp beds and reefs. Leopard sharks often follow the tide onto shallow-sloped shorelines to forage for food on the seabed.

Leopard sharks capture their prey by sucking water in with their mouths. This sucks up the food, which is then gripped by the teeth.

Leopard sharks are a target for fishermen, who catch them to sell as food. Live leopard sharks are also sold for keeping in aquariums.

Skin
The silvery-bronze skin is patterned with dark ovals that stretch in a neat row across the back.

Profile

Length:	28–47 in (males), 43–59 in (females)
Weight:	Up to 42 lb maximum (males and females)
Order:	Ground sharks
Family:	Hound sharks
Diet:	Bony fish, crabs, clams, shrimps (right), worms

Mouth

The mouth is on the flat underside of its head, and it opens downward. This is perfect for a shark that skims over the sand to pluck up crabs, clams, and worms.

Location

The leopard shark is found in shallow temperate (50–64 °F) water along the Pacific coast of North America. They swim from the shallows to about 295 feet deep.

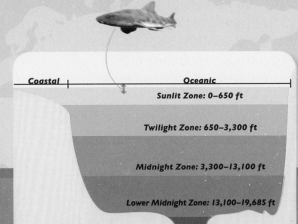

Coastal | Oceanic

Sunlit Zone: 0–650 ft

Twilight Zone: 650–3,300 ft

Midnight Zone: 3,300–13,100 ft

Lower Midnight Zone: 13,100–19,685 ft

NURSE SHARK

The nurse shark is one of the more docile types of shark. It is fairly lazy during the day, resting in groups on the bottom of the sea. It starts moving at night, which is when it hunts for food.

Nurse sharks are yellowish tan to dark brown in color. Young sharks sometimes have small black spots and bands on their skin.

They like warm water and live near the bottom in the shallows, sometimes close to mud or sand flats.

Unlike some sharks, nurse sharks can breathe without having to move through the water. Their respiratory system pumps water over the gills while they rest during the day.

Nurse sharks are bottom feeders. They use their sensitive barbels to search for food in the sand and silt on the ocean floor. They suck up food like a vacuum cleaner, rather than having to grasp it with their teeth.

Barbels
Thin, whisker-like organs on the lower jaw, called barbels, help the shark to find food in the sand and mud of the sea floor.

Profile

Length:	Average 6.9 ft (males), average 7.9 ft (females)
Weight:	200–265 lb (males) and 165–231 lb (females)
Order:	Carpet sharks
Family:	Nurse sharks
Diet:	Fish including rays, squid, octopus, crabs, small invertebrates

Tail fin
An extremely long tail fin makes up about a quarter of the shark's length.

Location

Nurse sharks are found in the tropical (more than 64 °F) waters of the western Atlantic and eastern Pacific Oceans. They swim from the shallows to about 230 feet deep.

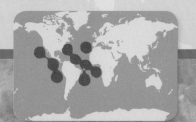

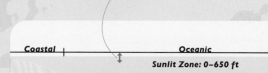

Coastal | Oceanic

Sunlit Zone: 0–650 ft

Twilight Zone: 650–3,300 ft

Midnight Zone: 3,300–13,100 ft

Lower Midnight Zone: 13,100–19,685 ft

COASTAL NURSERIES

Many animals visit coastal waters to breed or to have their young. These shallow waters are often sheltered, and there is plenty of food for the young animals.

Hammerhead sharks gather to breed.

Hammerhead gathering

Each year, hammerhead sharks gather together in special breeding places. Each male selects a female, and they then mate. After about 10 months, the female swims into shallow water to give birth to her pups.

DISCOVERY FACT™

The yearly migration of gray whales from Baja California nurseries to the Arctic feeding grounds and back is a distance of about 12,500 miles—the longest journey made by any mammal.

Whale migration

Many whales make regular journeys along the world's coasts. Humpback whales spend the summer in cold waters, where there is plenty of food. They then travel, or migrate, to warmer, shallow water, where the females give birth to their young.

Underwater flier

Manta rays live in the deep sea but give birth in shallow coastal waters, where the young stay for several years. The females are pregnant for about a year before giving birth to one or two pups.

REEF SHARKS

Coral reefs are some of the most colorful places on the planet. They are found in shallow, tropical waters and are home to thousands of different creatures. Several species of reef shark hunt in these waters, preying on fish and other marine animals.

WHERE IN THE WORLD?

Coral reefs are found in warm seas, where the water is shallow and there is plenty of light. Coral will grow only in clean water that is free from pollution.

Reef sharks live in tropical waters and lagoons near coral reefs.

Coral is made of polyps. These are tiny animals with tentacles, a little like sea anemones.

Reef sharks

Reef sharks are the top predators in their part of the oceans. Scientists know that if reef sharks are healthy and present in good numbers, the health of the reef and the fish that live on it must be good, too.

Great Barrier Reef

The Great Barrier Reef is the world's largest coral reef. It runs along the northeast coast of Australia and is 1,550 miles long. Almost 6,000 different species of animal live on this reef.

DISCOVERY FACT™

The Great Barrier Reef is the largest structure made by living creatures on Earth. It is so large that it can even be seen from space.

Reefs around the world

Most coral reefs are found in the Indian and Pacific Oceans, the Caribbean, and the Red Sea. Corals are not found where there are cold ocean currents or where large rivers flow into the sea.

Greenland

Arctic Ocean

ASIA

NORTH AMERICA

EUROPE

Atlantic Ocean

AFRICA

Pacific Ocean

Pacific Ocean

SOUTH AMERICA

Indian Ocean

AUSTRALIA

Coral reefs

Southern Ocean

LIVING REEF

Coral reefs are built by hard corals. These are coral animals that leave behind a stony skeleton when they die. Their skeletons create a habitat in which other animals can live.

Coral polyps

Tiny builders

Reefs are made by groups of tiny coral animals that live together. Each tiny coral animal is called a polyp. A polyp has a tubelike body and a ring of tentacles around its mouth. A reef is made up of millions of polyps all living together in one colony and held together by the stony skeleton.

Living in crevices

Many animals, such as the moray eel, hide in the cracks and crevices on the reef. The moray eel darts out and grabs any small fish that swim too close.

Feather star

Feather stars are related to starfish and live on the coral reef. They have a cup-shaped body and many feathery arms. The arms are covered in a sticky substance that traps small animals as they float by.

Feather star

Hunting fish

Reef sharks are clever hunters. They have found a way of herding shoals of fish against the faces of reefs. The fish cannot swim away, so are more easy to catch and eat.

Snapper fish live on the reef. Big reef sharks eat fish like this.

Vase sponges

Sponges

Sponges are animals, but they do not move around. Some sponges grow to about 6.5 feet tall. Others form a flat, crustlike growth over the surface of the reef. There are more than 5,000 different types of sponge. Some of the largest may be many hundreds of years old.

REEF SHARKS

Sharks are among the most feared animals on the reef.
Large reef sharks cruise along the reef edge looking for fish,
while smaller sharks hunt shrimps and crabs among the corals.

Blacktip reef shark

Blacktip reef sharks are not hunted by
any other animals. This shark hunts in
shallow water and lagoons. It catches
sea snakes as well as fish and octopuses.

Whitetip reef shark

The whitetip reef shark is browny gray
in color, but has white tips on its fins.
It rests during the day and hunts for food
at night in the crevices of the coral reef.

Zebra sharks

Zebra sharks live on the reef. Adults have
spots, but when they are young they have
stripes, just like a zebra. Their downward-
pointing mouth is designed to pick up
clams from the seabed. They also hunt
crabs and small fish.

A whitetip reef shark
rests under a
coral ledge.

DISCOVERY FACT™

Blacktip reef sharks sometimes bite off the legs of people who are wading through shallow water. Some experts think it is safer to swim through the shallows, rather than wading.

Blacktip reef sharks have distinctive black markings on the ends of their fins.

Gray reef shark

Gray reef sharks are very aggressive fish. If a diver gets too close, the shark will perform a threat display, warning that it is about to attack. It hunches its back and makes a side-to-side movement in the water.

BLACKTIP REEF SHARK

Fast-swimming and active, the blacktip reef shark is one of the three most common sharks inhabiting coral reefs in the tropical waters of the Indian Ocean and the western and central Pacific Ocean. It is mostly found in shallow inshore waters.

These streamlined sharks are brownish-gray on their upper surfaces and white underneath.

They are fast and active hunters, pursuing small fish and invertebrates back and forth around the reef. The patch of water in which they hunt is fairly small in size, and they do not stray far from these home waters, often staying in the same area for years at a time. Most blacktip reef sharks are found near rocky ledges and sandy flats, though they have also been known to swim into brackish (partly salty) water and even into freshwater near the sea.

This shark is fairly timid and does not pose a serious threat to humans. However, it has been known to bite people that come close when swimming, and particularly when wading, in shallow water.

Head
The snout is short and blunt, the eyes are oval, and the mouth is filled with narrow, saw-edged teeth.

Fins
All the fins have black or dark brown tips. This is highlighted on the dorsal fin, which has a light band beneath it.

Profile

Length:	5.2–5.9 ft (males and females)
Weight:	Up to 31 lb maximum (males and females)
Order:	Ground sharks
Family:	Requiem sharks
Diet:	Small fish, squid, shrimps, octopuses (right)

Tail
A sickle-shaped tail fin, built for speed, propels the blacktip reef shark through the water.

Location
Blacktip reef sharks are found in the shallow tropical (more than 64 °F) waters of the Indian and Pacific Oceans and the eastern Mediterranean Sea. They swim from the shallows to about 230 feet deep.

Coastal	Oceanic
	Sunlit Zone: 0–650 ft
	Twilight Zone: 650–3,300 ft
	Midnight Zone: 3,300–13,100 ft
	Lower Midnight Zone: 13,100–19,685 ft

CARIBBEAN REEF SHARK

The Caribbean reef shark is one of the most common sharks in the Caribbean. It is most active at night when it hunts for fish and invertebrates to eat.

A Caribbean reef shark has the muscular, streamlined shape that is typical of requiem sharks. It has a dark gray to gray-brown back, and white to light yellow stomach.

Caribbean reef sharks live near coral reefs and ocean bottoms near the continental and island shelves. They prefer shallow waters with a maximum depth of 100 feet. They are often found on the outer edges of coral reefs and sometimes even lying motionless on the ocean floor.

They feed mainly on small fish, which they grasp in the corner of the mouth. They use a sudden sideways snap of the jaws.

Some people stage shark feeds for tourists. Critics claim that this changes the natural balance of the food chain—the sharks may start to see humans as reliable sources of food, increasing the chances of a shark attack on humans.

Fins
The tips of the lower fins are dark, as are the rear edges of the large tail fin.

Profile

Length:	5–5.5 ft (males) and up to 10 ft (females)
Weight:	Up to 154 lb maximum (males and females)
Order:	Ground sharks
Family:	Requiem sharks
Diet:	Fish including rays, invertebrates such as octopuses and squid

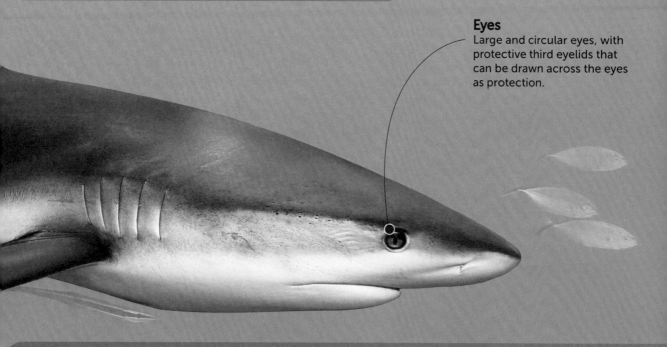

Eyes
Large and circular eyes, with protective third eyelids that can be drawn across the eyes as protection.

Location
Caribbean reef sharks are found in the shallow tropical (more than 64 °F) waters of the western Atlantic Ocean, as far south as northern Brazil. These streamlined sharks swim from the shallows to about 100 feet deep.

Coastal		Oceanic
		Sunlit Zone: 0–650 ft
		Twilight Zone: 650–3,300 ft
		Midnight Zone: 3,300–13,100 ft
		Lower Midnight Zone: 13,100–19,685 ft

LIVING TOGETHER

Animals live closely together on the reef. Some depend on others for a home, to stay clean, or for protection from predators.

Keeping a balance

Healthy coral reefs need sharks. Without sharks, large reef fish seriously reduce the numbers of algae-eating fish. The coral then suffers because too much algae on a reef kills it.

Cleaning station

Fish have difficulty removing the tiny parasites that live on their body, so they visit "cleaning stations" on the reef. Here, small fish and cleaner shrimps remove and eat the parasites for them.

Caribbean reef shark

Clown fish

Decorator crabs attach sponges and seaweeds to their shell. These living decorations help to disguise the crab from predators.

Living with stings

Anemones are covered in sting cells. Most animals stay away, but not the clown fish. It is able to live safely among the tentacles, as it is covered with a slimy mucus that protects it.

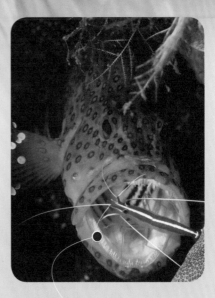

A coral grouper fish is cleaned by cleaner shrimps.

Living camouflage

The hermit crab protects its soft body by living inside an empty shell. Anemones have attached themselves to this hermit crab's shell. The anemones provide the crab with camouflage and protection, and in return, the crab helps the anemones to find food.

Cleanup

The coral grouper fish opens its mouth so that a cleaner shrimp can remove parasites from every nook and cranny. The shrimp gets a meal, and the fish gets rid of parasites.

WHITETIP REEF SHARK

One of the most common sharks found around coral reefs in the Indian and Pacific Oceans, the whitetip reef shark is typically found on or near the bottom in clear water.

During the day, whitetip reef sharks spend much of their time resting inside caves or even out in the open, lying on the seabed. Unlike other requiem sharks, which must constantly swim to breathe, the whitetip can lie still on the bottom without fear of drowning, as it can pump water over its gills.

At night, whitetips start to hunt. Their bodies are ideal for wriggling their way into gaps in the reef in pursuit of fish. They sometimes break off pieces of the coral in their eagerness to snatch the prey. Their target fish are beyond the reach of other species of shark that feed in open water. For this reason, whitetips are able to live alongside other species of reef shark without competing for the same sources of food.

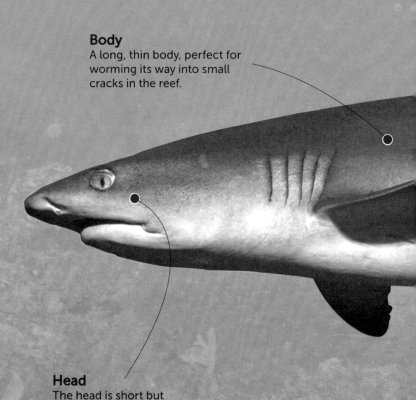

Body
A long, thin body, perfect for worming its way into small cracks in the reef.

Head
The head is short but broad, with whisker-like skin flaps beside the nostrils, called barbels.

Profile

Length:	3.6–5.2 ft (males and females)
Weight:	Up to 40 lb maximum (males and females)
Order:	Ground sharks
Family:	Requiem sharks
Diet:	Fish, octopuses, crabs, spiny lobsters (right)

Fins
Prominent white tips on the first dorsal fin and the tail fin give the whitetip reef shark its name.

Location
Whitetip reef sharks are found in the shallow tropical and subtropical (more than 64 °F) waters of the Indian and Pacific Oceans and along the western coast of Central America. They swim from the shallows to about 130 feet deep.

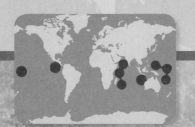

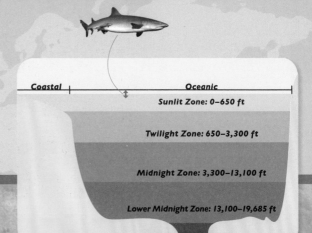

Coastal | Oceanic

Sunlit Zone: 0–650 ft

Twilight Zone: 650–3,300 ft

Midnight Zone: 3,300–13,100 ft

Lower Midnight Zone: 13,100–19,685 ft

OUT AT NIGHT

The reef is active at night because many of the animals are nocturnal. They hide during the day in caves and crevices, then come out to feed in the safety of the dark.

Cardinal fish

Whitetip reef shark

This shark mostly rests during the day, often lying with other whitetips. It becomes active at night when it hunts for food. It likes prey that live on the seabed in caves and crevices in the reef, especially octopuses, crabs, lobsters, fish, and eels.

Cardinal fish

The female cardinal fish lays her eggs in the water, where they are fertilized by the male. The male then collects them in his mouth and cares for them until they hatch. He releases the young fish in the safety of darkness.

Safety in numbers

Snappers are seen at night swimming around in small groups. They hunt crabs, shrimps, worms, and fish that live on sandy seabeds near reefs.

DISCOVERY FACT.™

The whitetip reef shark's thick skin protects it from getting cuts and grazes when bumping into the sharp coral.

Whitetip reef shark

Squirrel fish

Squirrel fish have extra-large eyes to help them see in low light conditions. The fish hide in caves and wrecked ships by day, then they come out at night to feed on plankton.

OCEAN SHARKS

Stretching beyond the coastal waters is the vast open ocean. It covers thousands of square miles of the Earth's surface and extends down for thousands of feet. Many different marine animals live in these huge stretches of water, including some of the strangest-looking, fiercest, and most amazing sharks of all.

WHALE SHARK

This is a true giant—the largest fish in the ocean. Despite its name, it is not a whale, but a gigantic shark that cruises slowly through the sea sucking in vast amounts of water as it filter-feeds.

The whale shark has distinctive light-yellow markings (random stripes and spots) dotted across its skin. Its skin can be up to 4 inches thick. The underlying color is usually dark gray, blue, or brown. Three large ridges run down each side of its body.

These sharks live in warm water, normally out in the open sea, although they do also come fairly close to shore. They are usually solitary feeders, swimming near the surface, where they scoop up vast amounts of plankton and small fish in their huge mouths. These are sieved out from the water using a technique called filter-feeding.

Whale sharks are quite harmless to humans. They are not worried by scuba divers coming close to them in the water.

Mouth
A huge gaping mouth vacuums up plankton and small fish.

Profile

Length:	20–40 ft (males and females)
Weight:	Typically around 16.5 tons (males and females), 22.5 tons maximum
Order:	Carpet sharks
Family:	Whale sharks
Diet:	Plankton (right), small fish, crustaceans

Gill slits
Large bristly gill rakers, behind each gill slit, filter particles of food from the water.

Location
Whale sharks are found worldwide in tropical (more than 64 °F) and warm temperate (50–64 °F) waters. They swim from the surface to 2,300 feet deep.

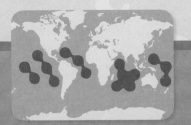

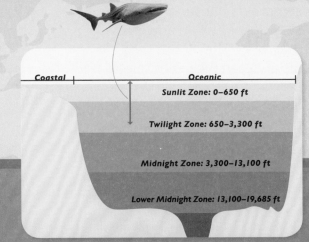

Coastal | Oceanic

Sunlit Zone: 0–650 ft

Twilight Zone: 650–3,300 ft

Midnight Zone: 3,300–13,100 ft

Lower Midnight Zone: 13,100–19,685 ft

BLUE SHARK

The blue shark is a long-distance traveler. It swims hundreds of miles every year, searching for food or to mate.

The blue shark has a bright blue back and a white stomach—these colors help to hide it in the ocean. Viewed from above, the deep blue blends with the murky waters; viewed from below, the white helps the shark to blend in with the light coming from above.

These large sharks hunt with their mouths wide open, trapping small fish, such as sardines, in their jaws. They also feed on squid and other invertebrates, such as octopuses and cuttlefish.

Blue sharks are slow swimmers but can move very quickly when attacking their prey. They travel long distances in their widespread habitat. One blue shark made a trip of over 4,000 miles from New York to Brazil!

Eyes
Large eyes are protected by a transparent third eyelid, which the shark can flick over the eyeball when it is hunting.

Tail
A long tail provides swimming power as the tail moves side-to-side.

Pectoral fins
Long pectoral fins—the same length as the distance between the tip of the snout and the last gill slit.

Profile

Length:	5.9–9.1 ft long (males), 7.2–10.8 ft long (females)
Weight:	60–121 lb (males), 205–401 lb (females)
Order:	Ground sharks
Family:	Requiem sharks
Diet:	Bony fish, squid, and other invertebrates

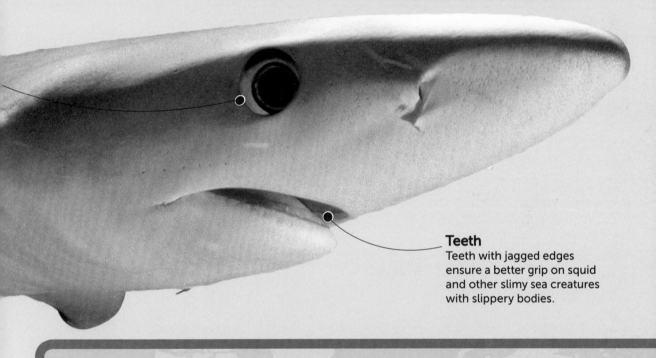

Teeth
Teeth with jagged edges ensure a better grip on squid and other slimy sea creatures with slippery bodies.

Location
Blue sharks are found worldwide in temperate (50–64 °F) waters and at lower depths in tropical (more than 64 °F) waters. They swim from the surface to about 1,150 feet deep.

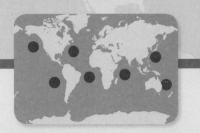

Coastal | Oceanic

Sunlit Zone: 0–650 ft

Twilight Zone: 650–3,300 ft

Midnight Zone: 3,300–13,100 ft

Lower Midnight Zone: 13,100–19,685 ft

GREAT HAMMERHEAD SHARK

There are nine species of hammerhead sharks, and the great hammerhead is the biggest of them. The shape of their head is unique.

Great hammerhead sharks are gray-brown to olive green on top with an off-white underside.

No one knows for sure why their head has such a strange shape. Scientists think that the extra distance between its eyes gives the shark a huge field of vision both above and below. Masses of special sensors on the underside of the "hammer" may allow it to detect the presence of stingrays when they are lying buried in the sand on the sea floor. Some hammerheads have even been seen to pin a stingray to the sea floor with their heads while they take a bite out of its wings to stop it escaping.

Great hammerheads migrate—they head to warmer waters during the winter and then return to their normal feeding grounds in summer.

Dorsal fin
A tall and pointed dorsal fin helps to stabilize the shark when it is turning quickly in the water as it hunts for prey.

Head
The head is shaped like a flattened hammer with the eyes set at the edges.

Tail

A tall tail fin made up of a large upper section, called a lobe, and a smaller lower section, propels the shark through the water.

Profile

Length:	13–20 ft (males and females)
Weight:	507–992 lb (males and females)
Order:	Ground sharks
Family:	Hammerhead sharks
Diet:	Fish, including rays (below) and other sharks, squid, octopuses, crustaceans

Location

Great hammerheads are found worldwide in tropical and subtropical (more than 64 °F) waters. They swim from the surface to about 262 feet deep.

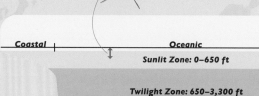

Coastal   *Oceanic*

Sunlit Zone: 0–650 ft

Twilight Zone: 650–3,300 ft

Midnight Zone: 3,300–13,100 ft

Lower Midnight Zone: 13,100–19,685 ft

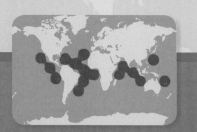

Scalloped hammerhead shark
This shark's name comes from the "scallops"
along the front edge of its hammer. These are
missing on other hammerhead sharks. The eyes
and nostrils are at the sides of the hammer.

OCEAN GIANTS

Pilot fish are often seen swimming alongside sharks. Both species benefit from this. The fish eat parasites off the skin of the sharks, while the shark scares away other predators that might eat the pilot fish.

Sharks share the oceans with other giant creatures, such as enormous whales, disk-shaped sunfish, and winged manta rays.

Oceanic whitetip shark

The oceanic whitetip shark grows to about 6.5 feet long. It swims just below the surface, but sometimes sticks its nose out of the water to sniff the air in search of food.

An oceanic whitetip shark with pilot fish swimming alongside it.

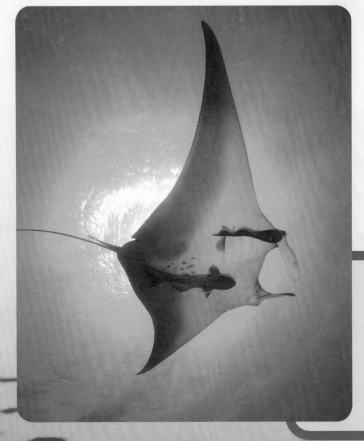

Manta ray

A manta ray usually swims slowly through the ocean, but when threatened by predators such as sharks, it leaps out of the water in an attempt to escape.

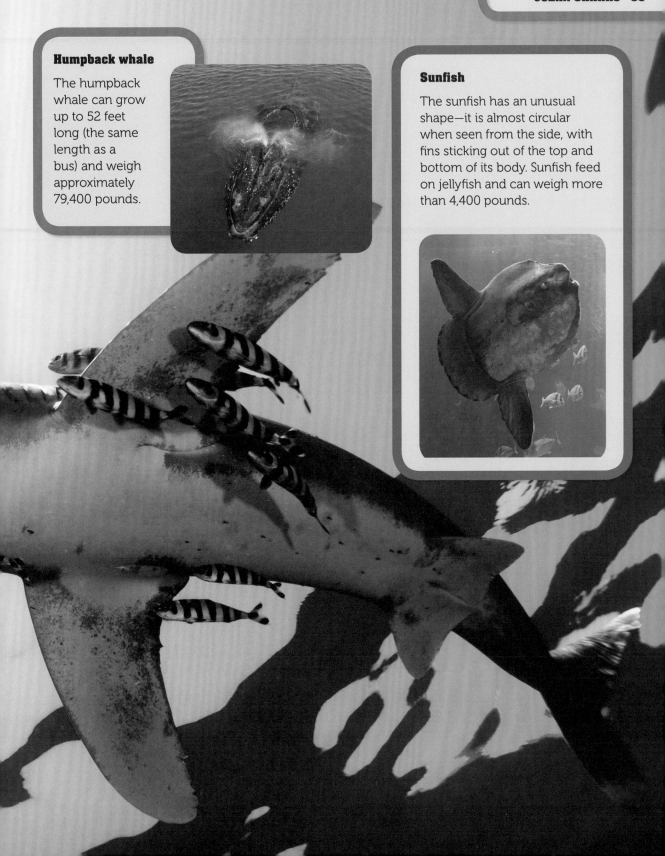

Humpback whale

The humpback whale can grow up to 52 feet long (the same length as a bus) and weigh approximately 79,400 pounds.

Sunfish

The sunfish has an unusual shape—it is almost circular when seen from the side, with fins sticking out of the top and bottom of its body. Sunfish feed on jellyfish and can weigh more than 4,400 pounds.

SILKY SHARK

This is one of the most common sharks in the open ocean. There are tens of millions of these slim, agile predators living in tropical waters around the world.

The back of the silky shark ranges in color from dark brown to a blue-gray. The underside is generally white, and the lower fins can have dark tips on their underside.

This shark usually hunts on it own and generally attacks fish swimming in open water. It is particularly attracted to tuna and is often seen trailing behind shoals of these fish. Sometimes, when there are lots of fish in the water, silky sharks will hunt together in a pack. They "herd" the shoal toward the surface. Then they slice into the shoal with their mouths open, to trap them in their jaws.

Silky sharks can act aggressively toward humans, but because they are normally found out in the open ocean, they do not often come into contact with divers.

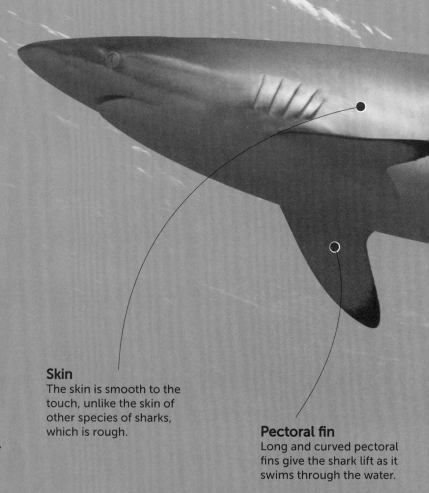

Skin
The skin is smooth to the touch, unlike the skin of other species of sharks, which is rough.

Pectoral fin
Long and curved pectoral fins give the shark lift as it swims through the water.

Dorsal fin
A short, rounded dorsal fin helps the silky shark balance.

Profile

Length:	5.9–6.9 ft (males), 6.9–7.5 ft (females)
Weight:	386–661 lb (males and females), 802 lb maximum
Order:	Ground sharks
Family:	Requiem sharks
Diet:	Fish (right), squid, crustaceans

Location
Silky sharks are found worldwide in tropical and subtropical waters, usually at a temperature of 73 °F or more. They swim from around 59 feet to about 1,640 feet deep.

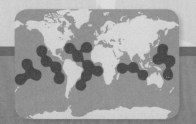

Coastal | Oceanic

Sunlit Zone: 0–650 ft

Twilight Zone: 650–3,300 ft

Midnight Zone: 3,300–13,100 ft

Lower Midnight Zone: 13,100–19,685 ft

OCEANIC WHITETIP SHARK

Oceanic whitetip sharks live in the open ocean. They often follow ships hoping to pick up scraps of food thrown overboard. For this reason, sailors used to call them "sea dogs."

The upper surface of the oceanic whitetip shark's body varies from grayish-bronze to brown in color, depending upon where it is in the world. The underside is whitish, sometimes with a yellow tinge.

The oceanic whitetip usually hunts alone and is quite slow-moving. It tends to cruise in the open ocean near to the surface. It covers vast stretches of empty water scanning for food. However, when it gets near its prey—usually fish or invertebrates—it can put on sudden bursts of speed.

When an oceanic whitetip senses the smell of blood in the water, it may go into a feeding frenzy, swimming around wildly and biting anything that comes near.

Oceanic whitetips are dangerous to humans because of their predatory nature. During World War II, they caused the deaths of many sailors and airmen who found themselves in the water after their ships were sunk or their aircraft were shot down.

Teeth
Sharp triangular upper teeth and smaller pointed lower teeth are ideal for holding and tearing the shark's prey.

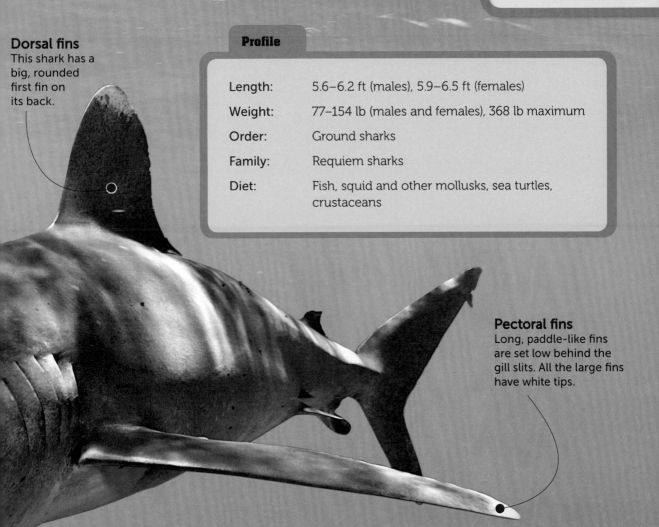

Dorsal fins
This shark has a big, rounded first fin on its back.

Profile

Length:	5.6–6.2 ft (males), 5.9–6.5 ft (females)
Weight:	77–154 lb (males and females), 368 lb maximum
Order:	Ground sharks
Family:	Requiem sharks
Diet:	Fish, squid and other mollusks, sea turtles, crustaceans

Pectoral fins
Long, paddle-like fins are set low behind the gill slits. All the large fins have white tips.

Location

Oceanic whitetip sharks are found worldwide in tropical waters, usually at a temperature between 68 and 82 °F. They swim from the surface to about 492 feet deep.

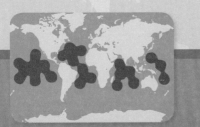

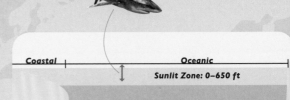

Coastal | Oceanic

Sunlit Zone: 0–650 ft

Twilight Zone: 650–3,300 ft

Midnight Zone: 3,300–13,100 ft

Lower Midnight Zone: 13,100–19,685 ft

SHARKS IN THE DEEP

Scientists have explored the upper layers of the sea quite thoroughly, but the deep ocean is still a mysterious place. We do not know much about this habitat. Few people have explored it by submarine. However, we do know that sharks live in deep water and can survive down to depths of around 10,000 feet.

GOING DOWN

As you descend from the surface, the sea becomes darker and colder. The pressure increases, too. In very deep water, a diver would be crushed and all the air squeezed from their lungs. Only animals adapted to this environment can survive. The surface layer goes down to about 650 feet. Next comes the twilight zone, from 650 to 3,300 feet. The midnight zone stretches to the seabed.

Sunlit zone

Sunlight passes through the water to depths of about 650 feet. Here in the surface layer, there is enough light for plant plankton and seaweeds to make their food.

Nurse sharks spend most of their time in the sunny surface layer of the sea.

Sixgill sharks are found down near the deep seabed.

Twilight zone

Beneath the surface layer, there is a glimmer of light—just enough for some animals to see. Animals dive down from the surface into this layer for safety.

Midnight zone

The midnight zone is pitch black and cold, and the water is still. Fish and other sea creatures living below 1,640 feet are designed to withstand the great pressure of the surrounding water.

Sperm whales can stay underwater for well over an hour without taking a breath.

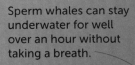

DISCOVERY FACT™

Sperm whales can dive to incredible depths. One sperm whale caught by a whaling ship in water 10,000 feet deep had a shark in its stomach.

Coastal	Oceanic
	Sunlit Zone: 0–650 ft
	Twilight Zone: 650–3,300 ft
	Midnight Zone: 3,300–13,100 ft
	Lower Midnight Zone: 13,100–19,685 ft

TWILIGHT ZONE

A variety of animals, from tiny plankton to huge whales, live permanently in the twilight zone. Their bodies are specially adapted for life in deep, gloomy water.

Cat sharks

Cat sharks are a family of around 150 species. These sharks live in habitats ranging from shallow waters right down to 6,560 feet or more. Some of them hunt in the twilight zone for nautilus, cuttlefish, and squid.

DISCOVERY FACT™

Frilled sharks live in deep waters in the twilight zone. They are shaped like a snake, with a huge mouth containing around 300 needle-like teeth.

Cat shark

Hatchet fish

A hatchet fish has a flat body. It has light-producing organs on its underside. The lights disguise the fish's shape so that it is not spotted by predators in the water below.

Twilight shrimp

The twilight shrimp has a red shell—a color that is difficult to spot in the gloom. It catches small plankton animals in its claws.

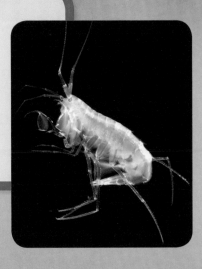

Nautilus

The nautilus is a relative of the squid. It has a spiral shell for protection. If necessary, it can disappear inside completely. Its eyes help it see in the gloom.

The nautilus has many more tentacles than a squid, but no suckers.

Eye

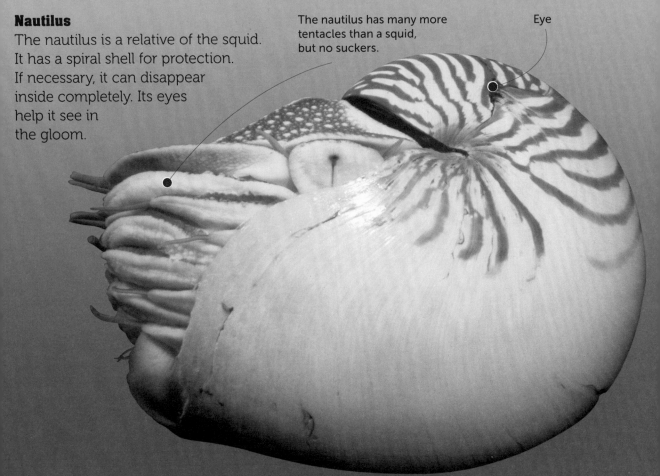

DIVING DEEP

Seals, whales, sharks, and penguins are just some of the animals that dive down into the twilight zone and beyond to find food.

Little is known about the megamouth shark, which was first discovered near Hawaii in 1976. Since then, only about 40 megamouths have been seen.

Megamouth

The odd-looking megamouth shark grows to about 23 feet long. It has a 3-foot-wide mouth. Like many ocean animals, it spends the daylight hours in deep water and swims to the surface to feed at night.

Diving birds

Many seabirds, such as penguins, dive underwater to catch food. The penguin is a flightless bird with flippers rather than wings. It is clumsy on land, but an expert swimmer. The emperor penguin spends up to 15 minutes under the water at a time. It dives to depths of about 1,640 feet.

Weddell seals

The Weddell seal dives at night to find krill, squid, and fish. It can stay under the water for up to an hour, reaching depths of about 2,300 feet before it has to return to the surface to breathe.

Weddell seal

Twilight hunter

The sperm whale dives down to 3,300 feet or more, in search of squid. Scientists believe that the whale produces sound waves to stun its prey.

GOBLIN SHARK

Very little is known about the goblin shark as it lives in the deep ocean. Only about 45 specimens have been studied to date.

Goblin sharks are not often seen because they live in deep water at the bottom of the ocean. They are only seen when they are caught in the fishing nets of deep-sea trawlers. The goblin shark is pink-gray in color because its blood vessels lie close to the surface of the skin and can be seen through it.

It is very dark in the deep ocean, so the goblin shark does not rely on its eyesight to detect prey. Scientists think that special organs on its long snout can detect the faint electrical fields created by other fish and invertebrates when they move. It may also use the snout to dig up fish and crustaceans that are hiding in the sand and silt on the seafloor.

A goblin shark's jaws act like a spring-loaded trap. The teeth and jaws can be catapulted forward, a little like opening a telescope, to snatch a fish from the water. Then they spring back to their normal position.

Body
The body is soft and quite rubbery. The caudal fin is very long compared to the two dorsal fins.

Profile

Length:	7.9–10.5 ft (males), 10–11.5 ft (females)
Weight:	Around 400 lb (males and females), 463 lb maximum
Order:	Mackerel sharks
Family:	Goblin sharks
Diet:	Fish, squid (right) and other mollusks, crustaceans

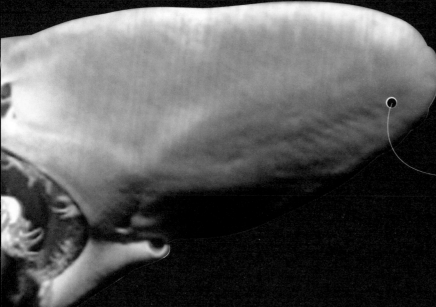

Snout
The large flattened snout protrudes from the top of its head. Beneath this are the jaws with slender, fanglike teeth.

Location
Goblin sharks have been found off the coast of Japan, Australia, New Zealand, and southern Africa, and in the eastern Atlantic and Indian Oceans. They swim near the sea bottom at about 820 feet deep, but they can go down to 1,650 feet or more.

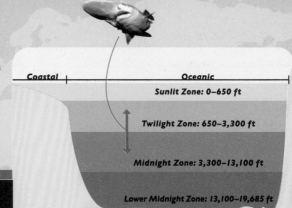

Coastal | Oceanic

Sunlit Zone: 0–650 ft

Twilight Zone: 650–3,300 ft

Midnight Zone: 3,300–13,100 ft

Lower Midnight Zone: 13,100–19,685 ft

THE DEEP

The deep is a cold, eerie place where very little lives. The animals of the deep have all kinds of unusual features that help them get something to eat in this "food desert."

Light in the dark

Sunlight does not penetrate the deep ocean. It is very dark all the time. Many animals in the deep-sea have developed organs that can produce light. This is known as bioluminescence. It is used to lure prey, to distract predators, and to attract mates.

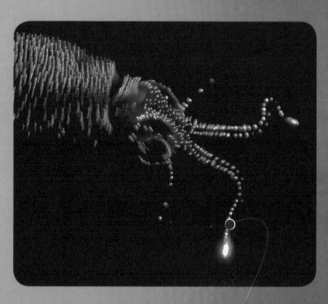

The firefly squid has tiny organs on its tentacles that emit light. This attracts small fish, which the squid eats.

Deep-sea medusa

The deep-sea medusa is a relative of the jellyfish. It traps prey, such as small shrimps and baby fish, in its long tentacles. It has 22 of them around its body.

Snipe eel

The snipe eel has jaws that do not close. It swims with its mouth open. Small animals, such as amphipods (shrimplike creatures), are trapped on the teeth and swallowed. The snipe eel grows to over 3 feet long.

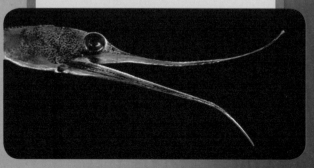

Scuba divers do not normally go deeper than around 131 feet. To explore the deep ocean, scientists use manned submersibles or robot vehicles.

DISCOVERY FACT

The velvet bel
shark can g
light. Its phot
(light-producir
are arranged in
pattern. This h
bellies recog
another in th

Fishing the deep

The anglerfish lures its prey with a light that dangles from the end of a spine in front of its large mouth. The light is produced by tiny bacteria.

SIXGILL SHARK

This big shark normally lives in the darkness of the deep oceans at depths down to around 6,560 feet.

The sixgill shark ranges in color from gray and olive green to brown on the upper side, fading to a paler underside. There is a light-colored stripe along each flank. It has small, teardrop-shaped, green eyes with black pupils.

It normally hunts on its own, swimming slowly and steadily through the water searching for food. When it spots something to eat, it accelerates rapidly to catch its prey. The teeth in its lower jaw are shaped like the blade of a saw. The shark uses them to rip the flesh off the body of large fish that it cannot swallow whole.

Sixgill sharks are not considered dangerous to humans because they are quite shy and not aggressive unless provoked. Also, they generally keep to deep waters where divers cannot follow them.

Gills
Most sharks have five gill slits on each side of their bodies, but the sixgill shark has six long slits.

Length:	10–10.8 ft long (males), 11.5–14 ft long (females)
Weight:	Average 440 lb (males), 880 lb (females), 1,300 lb maximum
Order:	Frilled and cow sharks
Family:	Cow sharks
Diet:	Fish, snails, crabs (right), shrimps, squid, some marine mammals

Dorsal fin

There is only one dorsal fin on this shark's back, set quite a long way back toward the tail.

Location

Sixgill sharks are found worldwide in tropical (over 64 °F) and temperate (50–64 °F) waters. They usually swim from about 295 feet to as deep as 6,560 feet.

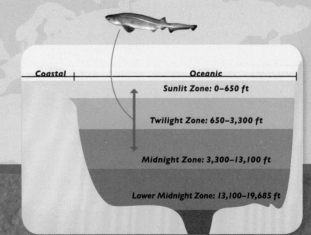

Coastal | Oceanic

Sunlit Zone: 0–650 ft

Twilight Zone: 650–3,300 ft

Midnight Zone: 3,300–13,100 ft

Lower Midnight Zone: 13,100–19,685 ft

FOOD AND SHELTER

When the body of a large animal drops to the seabed, scavengers come from far and wide to feed upon it. Other animals take shelter among objects that find their way to the seabed.

There is a constant supply of "marine snow" from the waters above. This "snow" is the broken-down remains of dead plants and animals—especially plankton. These tiny remains drift slowly to the seabed where they become an important source of food for bottom-dwellers.

Spiny dogfish shark

Finding shelter

Animals on the seabed need shelter from predators. Many hide among bones—or even old cans and objects that have dropped to the seabed. Unfortunately, deep-sea trawling nets can sweep away these tiny shelters.

DISCOVERY FACT™

Sharks usually eat live prey rather than scavenging on the seafloor. But the spiny dogfish shark is a bottom-dwelling scavenger. It has two sharp poisonous spines on its back to keep other predators away.

Hagfish

The hagfish looks
something like an eel. It
is a scavenger that lives
on the ocean floor. The
hagfish burrows into the
bodies of dead animals
and eats them from
the inside out. It is an
unusual fish because it
does not have jaws or
teeth. Instead, it has a
very rough tongue.

Brittle star

The brittle star has five
long arms, which it uses
to pull itself across the
seabed. It sometimes
preys on small shrimps
and other animals, but
it mostly scavenges on
dead matter.

DEEP-OCEAN CLIFFS

There are cliffs, mountains, and trenches in the deep ocean.
These are home to many animals, including corals and sponges.

Deep-sea coral

Not all corals are found in
shallow, warm, tropical seas.
Many corals live in cold,
deep water. Some live as
deep as 3,300 feet. Deep-sea
reefs grow very slowly,
and some are hundreds of
years old.

Deep-sea coral

Deep-sea sponges

Some deep-water
sponges have a skeleton
that is made from glass.
They produce tiny
pieces of glass, which
stick together to form a
beautiful skeleton that
is strong enough to
support their body.

Hiding in cracks

The wolffish, or sea wolf, pushes its body
backward into the cracks of a cliff. It leaves
its head sticking out, watching for prey. It has a
wide mouth with large pointed teeth, which it
uses to feed on clams, mussels, and starfish.

A wolffish hides in a
hole in the rocks.

Cliff hugger

Sea anemones, and other animals that cannot swim, cling tightly to the cliff. If they let go, they could sink into the deep below.

Divers can explore cliffs that lie close to the surface. Mini-submarines are needed for the deep ocean.

DISCOVERY FACT™

The Portuguese shark holds the world record for the deepest-caught shark. Most live at around 3,300 feet, but several have been caught down at around 9,840 feet.

SHARKS AND PEOPLE

Although sharks have been living in the Earth's oceans for more than 400 million years, in recent years their future has become threatened. This is because human beings have started to affect what happens to creatures in the ocean, leading to a serious decline in the number of sharks.

SHARK FISHING

Many sharks are known as apex predators. This means that they kill and eat other animals, but that virtually no predators in the oceans kill them. However, sharks do have one deadly enemy that lives on land—humans.

Commercial fishing

Every year, around 100 million sharks are caught and killed. This is because a lot of people earn their living by catching sharks. Shark products, including meat, the fins, the skin, and the teeth, are sold in huge quantities.

Unwanted victims

Sharks are often caught in trawler nets or on longline hooks that have been set to catch other fish, such as tuna or swordfish. The sharks die, even though the fisherman do not want them. They are known as "by-catch."

Sport fishing

In certain parts of the world, the sport of fishing for big game fish is very popular. Some fishermen release the fish after it has been caught and photographed, but others kill their catch to keep as a trophy.

Sharks are one of the game fish that sport fisherman try to catch using fast boats like this.

Shark's fin soup

A thick soup made from shark fins is very popular in the Far East. It is thought to have medicinal properties. Some fishermen catch sharks, cut off their fins, and then throw the sharks back in the water. Millions die in this way.

GETTING CLOSE TO SHARKS

Many people are curious about sharks—they are big, powerful, and fascinating animals. There are different ways that we can see them up-close.

Diving with sharks

In the clear, warm waters of the tropics, diving with sharks has become a tourist attraction. Some dive companies even organize shark feeds to attract sharks to a particular spot.

In the aquarium

One way that people can get close to sharks is to visit one of the many aquariums that display them to the public. As well as providing a tourist attraction, these sea life centers allow scientists to study shark behavior in order to help protect them.

DISCOVERY FACT™

The Ocean Voyager tank at Georgia Aquarium in Atlanta, Georgia, is the largest aquarium habitat in the world. It contains more than 6 million gallons of salt water—large enough to be a home for whale sharks.

Shark cages

The great white shark is seen as the ultimate man-eater. It is now possible for tourists to watch great whites from inside the safety of a submerged metal cage.

Great white shark

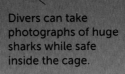

On the screen

Television has had a huge impact on our knowledge of sharks. Nature programs give us an insight into their behavior and habits. Movies such as *Jaws* and *Deep Blue Sea* portray the shark as a deadly monster.

Divers can take photographs of huge sharks while safe inside the cage.

GREAT WHITE SHARK

The huge and aggressive great white is the most dangerous shark in the world. It has attacked more swimmers, surfers, divers, and small boats than any other species of shark.

A great white shark's body is streamlined and shaped like a torpedo. Despite its name, only its belly is actually white; the top is gray or blue-gray. This is useful when hunting its prey because the great white usually strikes from below—to its prey above, its gray color blends in with the dark water.

The shark's target is normally attacked in a surprise rush and bitten once to stun it. Sometimes, the shark will leap out of the water because of the speed and power of its attack. When the victim is stunned and dying, the shark returns to feed.

The great white is the only shark that pokes its head out of the water. It may be to spot prey swimming on the surface, such as seals and sea lions.

Pectoral fins
Large sickle-shaped pectoral fins help the shark to steer through the water.

Profile

Length: 11.5–13 ft (males), 15–16.5 ft (females), 22 ft maximum

Weight: Average 1,500–4,000 lb (males and females), 7,000 lb maximum

Order: Mackerel sharks

Family: Mackerel sharks

Diet: Fish including other sharks, seals, sea lions, dolphins, small whales, sea turtles

Nostrils
An incredible sense of smell can detect one drop of blood in 26 gallons of water and sense blood up to 3 miles away.

Teeth
Around 300 huge, triangular, jagged teeth—each one as long as a human finger.

Location
Great white sharks are found worldwide in temperate (50–64 °F) waters, and some also are found in tropical (over 64 °F) waters. They swim from the surface to 6,600 feet.

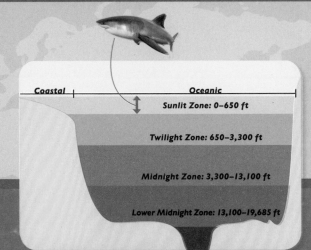

Coastal | Oceanic

Sunlit Zone: 0–650 ft

Twilight Zone: 650–3,300 ft

Midnight Zone: 3,300–13,100 ft

Lower Midnight Zone: 13,100–19,685 ft

SHARK ATTACKS

Whenever a shark attacks someone swimming offshore, it makes news all around the world, particularly if the victim is killed. But most experts agree that the risk of being attacked by a shark is very small.

Attacks are rare

Worldwide, there are only around 70 to 100 attacks in an average year, of which around 10 to 15 are fatal. More people are killed by bees each year than by sharks.

Surfing star

In October 2003, 13-year-old Bethany Hamilton was surfing off the coast of Hawaii when she was attacked by a tiger shark. It bit off her left arm. She survived the attack and returned to the water 26 days later. In 2007, she became a professional surfer.

When sharks attack surfers, they probably mistake the outline of the surfboard for prey.

Survivor

One of world's leading authorities on the great white shark, Rodney Fox, was himself the victim of a terrible attack in 1963. He was almost bitten in half and his wounds needed more than 450 stitches. Since then, he has dedicated his life to the appreciation and preservation of the great white shark.

A fighting chance

Anyone who is unlucky enough to be attacked by a shark should try to fight back by hitting the shark on its snout and clawing at its eyes and gills.

The eyes and snout are a shark's vulnerable areas.

Great white shark
A great white breaks the surface of the water as it hunts for food. These are the largest predatory fish in the oceans. Their bite is about twice as powerful as that of a lion.

SHORTFIN MAKO SHARK

This is one of the fastest sharks in the ocean. It can reach speeds of up to 30 miles per hour when chasing after prey and can leap clear out of the water to heights of up to 20 feet.

The shortfin mako shark's upper side is metallic blue while the underside is white. This pattern is known as countershading. It makes the shark hard to spot in the water when seen both from above and from below.

The shortfin mako's speed allows it to feed on quick-moving fish, such as tuna, swordfish, and even other sharks. It is able to hunt them because it swims faster than they do.

Due to their size and speed, shortfin makos can be dangerous to humans. There have been a number of attacks on swimmers and divers, and some of them have been fatal. Divers have reported that the shark will swim in a figure-of-eight pattern before launching an attack with its mouth open.

Body shape
Sleek and streamlined with a long, cone-shaped snout. It slips easily through the water, which helps the shark to swim so fast.

Profile

Length:	Average 5.9–8.2 ft (males and females), 12.8 ft maximum
Weight:	Average 132–300 lb (males and females), 1,250 lb maximum
Order:	Mackerel sharks
Family:	Mackerel sharks
Diet:	Fish including other sharks, rays, squid, dolphins (right), small whales

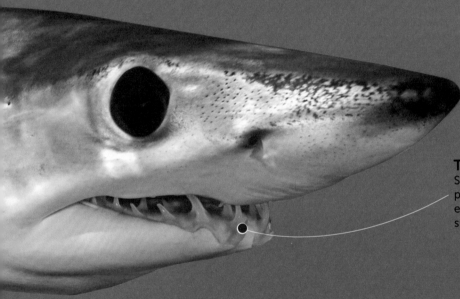

Teeth

Slender, slightly curved, and pointed teeth, with razor-sharp edges, help the mako grip slippery, fast-moving fish.

Location

Shortfin mako sharks are found worldwide in warm temperate (16 to 64 °F) and tropical (over 64 °F) waters. They swim from the surface to around 500 feet.

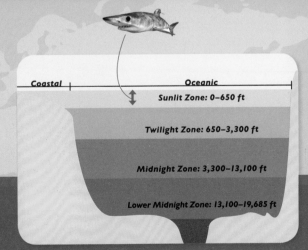

Coastal | Oceanic

Sunlit Zone: 0–650 ft

Twilight Zone: 650–3,300 ft

Midnight Zone: 3,300–13,100 ft

Lower Midnight Zone: 13,100–19,685 ft

GLOBAL WARMING

Global warming is the gradual increase in temperature of the Earth's atmosphere. Scientists believe that this will cause climates to change, sea levels to rise, and extreme weather to become more common.

Changing habits

As the sea gets warmer, some marine animals change their behavior. They appear in places where they have not been seen before. Scientists believe that some time this century sharks will begin to be seen in the ocean around Antarctica.

Reefs in danger

Warming seas around coral reefs can cause devastation. The coral dies and turns white. This deprives reef fish of food and shelter, and their population drops. This, in turn, means that the reef sharks struggle to find food.

Polluting the atmosphere

Global warming is thought to be caused by an increase in greenhouse gases such as carbon dioxide. These gases trap heat in the atmosphere. Carbon dioxide is produced when oil, gas, and coal are burned.

What can we do?

Everybody can help to slow down global warming by walking and cycling because this does not burn oil. If we travel in airplanes, buses, or cars, carbon dioxide is produced, which may speed up global warming.

Beautiful natural habitats like this coral reef are threatened by rising sea temperatures.

PROTECTING SHARKS

Although changes in the world's weather, the effects of pollution, and the impact of fishing all spell danger for sharks, many people are trying to protect and conserve shark populations around the globe.

Shark sanctuaries

Some countries have banned commercial fishing in their national waters (the parts of the sea that they control), to help protect sharks. The island groups of Palau, in the western Pacific Ocean, and the Maldives, in the Indian Ocean, have both done this.

Palau, a country made up of around 250 Pacific islands, has created a protected area for sharks.

Acting responsibly

Tourists who want to see and swim with sharks should make sure that the dive company treats sharks with proper care.

How can we help?

We can help sharks survive in the wild by not buying shark products, which encourages shark fishing. We can also try to persuade politicians to change the laws that govern how commercial fishing is done. Some people are trying to get laws changed so that sharks are better protected.

Better understanding

Scientific research, sea life visitor centers, television programs, magazine articles, movies, and books all help the general public to understand that sharks are remarkable creatures.

Scientists tag a shortfin mako shark, to help track its migrations.

DISCOVERY FACT™

Scientists in New Zealand have tagged a mako shark so that it can be tracked by satellite. It traveled more than 8,260 miles in 7 months, sometimes swimming more than 60 miles in a day.

Aquariums are great places to learn about sharks and see them close up.

Whale shark
A whale shark glides through the water surrounded by smaller fish and almost as many scuba divers.